Miriam's Iris
or
Angels
In the Garden

Poetry by
Maja Trochimczyk

ALSO BY MAJA TROCHIMCZYK

POETRY

Rose Always – A Court Love Story
Gloria and Assorted Praises

MUSIC HISTORY

After Chopin: Essays in Polish Music
The Music of Louis Andriessen
Polish Dance in Southern California

FORTHCOMING

Spatial Music: A History
A Romantic Century in Polish Music
The Nightingale in Space: Essays on Music
Paderewski: Portraits of a Musician

Miriam's Iris

or

Angels in the Garden

Poetry by
Maja Trochimczyk

Moonrise Press, 2008

Moonrise Press

Moonrise Press

P.O. Box 4288
Los Angeles – Sunland
CA 91041-4288
www.moonrisepress.com

Prior publication of certain poems from this collection in the
following collections is hereby gratefully acknowledged: Poems *Eloe
1-3. Amor 1, In Passing 6*, and *Ellenai 2* appear in *Sunlight Confessions*
(KRAK Group, Los Angeles, 2008); *Rivers* in *poeticdiversity*, August
2008; *Waterfalls* and *Timelessness* in chapbooks by Poets on Site,
Pasadena (April, September 2008).

Photos © 2001-2008 by Maja Trochimczyk
Author's photo © 2008 by Andrzej Kolodziey

Design and layout by Maja Trochimczyk using fonts:
        Papyrus (titles), Arial and Garamond (poems)

The Library of Congress Publication Data:

Trochimczyk, Maja, 1957–
    [Poems. English. Collections]
    Miriam's Iris, or Angels in the Garden / Maja Trochimczyk
        110 pp. 15.2 x22.9cm.
        Written in English.
        ISBN 978-0-578-00166-1 (perfect bound; alk. paper)
        I. Trochimczyk, Maja, 1957–Poetry. II. Title.

10 9 8 7 6 5 4 3 2 1

... through fire and water ... to freedom

Psalm 66:12

Preface

The genesis of this collection includes years of travelling and an internal journey leading to a serene California garden. The map of the stages of this journey is created by the appearances of six angels: Amor, the angel of romance, Eros, the angel of desire, Eloe, the angel of sorrow, Thanatos, the angel of death, Ellenai, the angel of consolation, and Sophia, the angel of timeless wisdom. Eros and Thanatos are Greek twins, Amor is their baby cousin. Eloe died of sorrow and Ellenai carried her on his wings in Juliusz Słowacki's romantic drama, *Anhelli*. Sophia needs no introductions, since she is the wise Queen, the best friend of Rumi and all Christian mystics.

In acknowledging my debt to my colleagues, predecessors, and fellow students of the subject, I should only say "thank you" for all they have done for me. My parents' subscription to literary weekly, *Życie Literackie* in Poland, started my poetic peregrinations from Wisława Szymborska's poetry column. My mother's abundant poetry collection, with Norwid, Mickiewicz and Poświatowska next to bilingual editions of Apollinaire and Rimbaud was a window into timelessness. Jacek bought my first Bible where I discovered the surreal and enchanting *Song of Songs*. Paweł gave me Miłosz and his translation of the Psalms (I gave him Rilke); Jim gave me e.e.cummings. Louis signed a dedication on a slim volume of the *Four Quartets* by T.S. Eliot, wondering when I'd stop obsessing about it. (The answer? Never.) Vince was Vince.

I thank poets from the Pasadena group Poets on Site led by Kath Abela Wilson for their comments that helped improve some of my verse gathered here. Kath, Justin Kibbe, Jane Engleman, Pauli Dutton, and Debbie P Kolodji have been particularly helpful with their insights. Finally, I'm grateful for the beauty found in the world, observed "in passing…"

Maja Trochimczyk
October 2008, Los Angeles

vii

CONTENTS:

Miriam's Iris ◊ 1
Prelude - Water Charms ◊ 3

In Passing 1 ◊ 9

Amor, the Angel of Romance ◊ 11

Interlude – Of the Mountains ◊ 22
In Passing 2 ◊ 25

Eros, the Angel of Desire ◊ 27

Interlude – Rivers ◊ 36
In Passing 3 ◊ 39

Eloe, the Angel of Grief ◊ 41

Interlude – Waterfalls ◊ 50
In Passing 4 ◊ 53

Thanatos, the Angel of Death ◊ 55

Interlude – Of Days ◊ 64
In Passing 5 ◊ 67

Ellenai, the Angel of Peace ◊ 69

Interlude – Of Bliss ◊ 78
In Passing 6 ◊ 81

Sophia, the Angel of Wisdom ◊ 83

In Passing 7 ◊ 93
Postlude – A Vision ◊ 95

Biographical Note ◊ 99

Miriam's Iris

Why did you want to look
into Miriam's iris?
Why did you want to catch her gaze
that silently unfolds
the petals of conceit,
self-pity, and bewilderment,
revealing bluest sorrow,
soft heart of gold?

Love is awakened lightly
sleeping it waits to be:
daily enchantment —

Swirls of transfigured glory
dancing a fragrant dream:
four million circles —

Prelude - Water Charms

I.

The hummingbird builds its nest.
Its thin beak – the stem
of a multicolored jewel
sparkling in the sun
(a copy of its own similitude) –
holds the glistening body aflutter.

Rose bushes wear diamonds,
well-polished – their colors change
with the breeze
like the bird's shiny feathers.

My Californian garden
tries to seduce me
with precious necklaces
and melliferous strains
from the mocking bird
hovering above
the scent of gardenias.

"All right" – I say –
 "Don't play games with me.
I've seen it all before."

II.

Pearls scattered on the meadow
tremble on the blades of grass,
hide in the hearts of clover.

The sun shines straight through their ovals,
translucent, in a bright shade of green.
Stalks bend under their glassy weight.

Tempted by curiosity,
I destroy their perfect balance,
depriving the world
of its well-deserved splendor.

The droplets fall
to the ground and disappear.

How shall I ever be forgiven?
My wickedness – unthinkable.

III.

Dead leaves seek shelter
under thin panes of glass.
Ice covers pools of rainwater.

The stillness mocks past intimacy
when noisy reds, yellows, and browns
flew up from under my feet
in an autumn park
of maples and poplars.

I changed the future of the world
with one step of my boot:
the pane cracked,
the air bubbles shifted,
the harmony was gone.

With glee I crushed the worlds
that did not need me.

I shudder when I look back –
a trail of footsteps
filled with muddy water,
dirt splattered on the geometry of ice.

IV.

The magic of white butterflies
twirling in the glow of street lamps
makes me dizzy. The black sky turns.
Bright spots move faster still.

I'm afraid. They chase me –
larger – whiter – denser
stars, monsters, snowflakes?

My scarlet fever began that night.

V.

Winter morning reveals its treasures.
Leaves, cones, twigs, tree-trunks,
even pebbles on my path
wear bristling coats of crystal ice.

The pearl-grey sky is a bride's dress,
waiting to burst open with new life.

The clouds settle on their beds.
Houses, bushes, roofs, fences,
dress in white muffs,
scarves and blankets.

The fence boards,
stiff like British soldiers,
present puffy hats to the Queen.

I admit it. I cut their heads off
with my red-gloved hand,
leaving behind a line
of headless corpses –
oh, silent horror!

VI.

The damage that cannot be undone –
melting the universe of beauty
with one breath
that changed a snowflake
into a dirty spot on my glove.

Slowly walking into
the immaculate field of whiteness,
I scarred the snow's pristine expanse
with clumsy footmarks.

VII.

Again: plunging into
the smooth expanse of a lake,
I broke its sleepy obsession
with mirroring the evening sky.

I paid for my guilt with exile –
a foreign country, a borrowed name.

Crystals do not charm me in the desert
where Joshua trees parody my gestures
of praying for snowflakes
by stretching their twisted limbs
into the purple sky.

No hope for *maki, chabry*, and *rumianki.*
My childhood flowers
won't be found on the meadow
painted yellow by the spring
across the barren slope
I see from my kitchen window.

VIII.

I've dreamt of being happy
in the sweet impossible,
with Italian cypresses, ice plants,
and a white fence around my house.

But my memories trap me.
Only the hummingbird
floats around, twitching its tail
like a miniature goldfish.

Maki – wild, red poppies (Papaver rhoeas); *chabry* – blue Centaurea cyanus, and *rumianki* – white chamomile daisies, grow in the meadows and fields of Poland and throughout central Europe.

In Passing 1

The bougainvillea looked at me slyly
from the myriad of her butterfly eyes

Roses sang with rich voices
of their crimson petals

A symphony unfolded to fade

My white birch was afraid
of this southern opulence

Its leaves trembled in the hot wind
far from the pale whisper of home

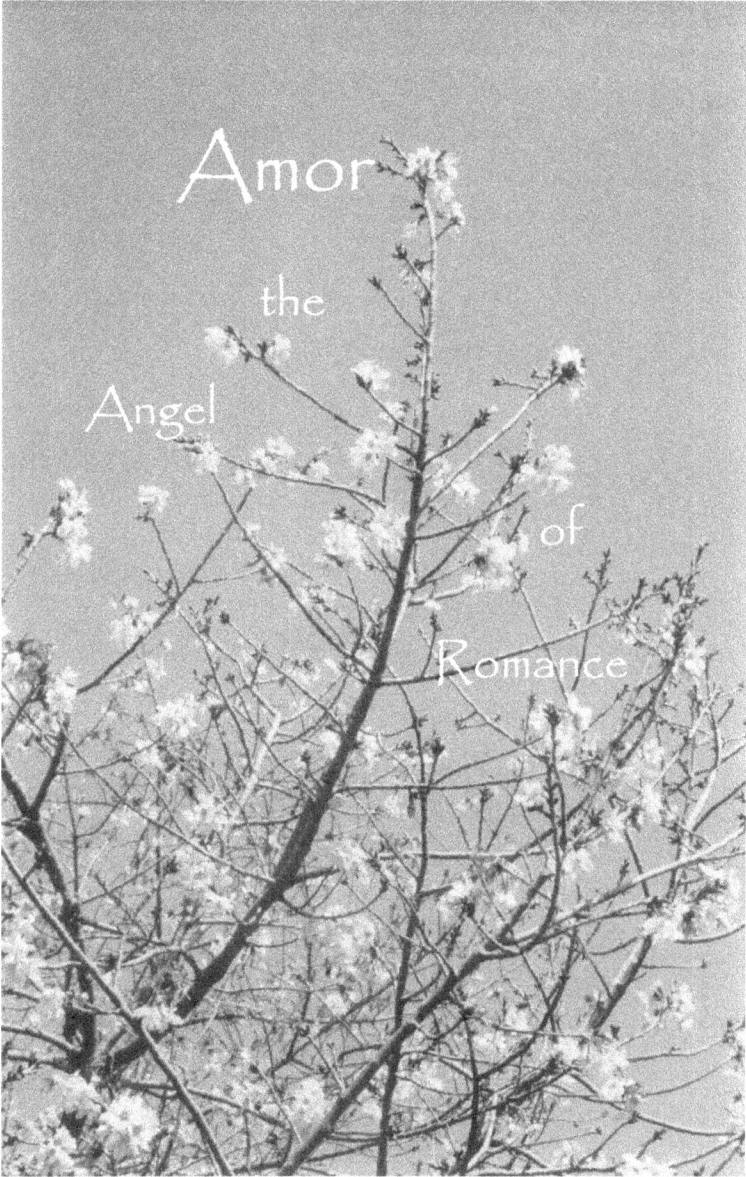

Amor
the
Angel
of
Romance

Amor 1

I wish I were a bluebird
outside your window –

I could watch you working, undisturbed

I wish I lived in the vastness
of truth and beauty –
hazel infinity of your kind eyes.

I wish I could kiss your fingers,
so strong and gentle –
warm hand resting on my frightened cheek

I wish you were my brother
from the *Song of Songs* –

our love – a blossom under almond sky

Amor 2

you looked at me
and I saw myself
for the first time

I'm beautiful!
I've heard this
many times before
but did not quite believe

In your hands
love filled every
square inch of my skin
I glow with a brightness
that even your absence
cannot dim

Amor 3

you touched a bell
with a trembling hand
that withdrew
from its cold indifference

yet the sound grew within
till stillness exploded
into a deafening noise
of freedom

this bell rings within me

Amor 4

it had to be the eleventh,
the time of perfect absence
of all time's measure,
the number so uncounted
that doubly prime –
the day of fullness

in a second there is a universe
never heard of;
in a glimpse – a mystery
fully apprehended

once for all understood

found and lost together

all times swirling
in a glorious wreath of the present

Augustine was right –
sometimes God
makes a hole in Heaven,
for us to peek in

Amor 5

water of the sun,
water of desire –
fruit-bowl of the fountain
overflows

tiny pearl-drops sparkle,
giggling through the air
with delight
equal to the bliss
of my skin caressed
by your dancing fingers

(funny, how we both assume
that there is – could be –
someone else
to break the harmony
of our love)

◊ ◊ ◊

praise the enormousness of guilt
washed away
by sparkling solar fountain

Amor 6

the more I love
the more dangerous
life becomes
in its graphic beauty
carved with a dagger
stolen from time

the blade cuts
old wounds open

it slides on the skin
of the moment

pierced by knowing

Interlude – Of the Mountains

I.

I love you, my mountains,
oranged into sunset
of embarrassment.

Your cheeks aglow –
what sin you're hiding,
in waterless creases,
what guilt?

Or is it first love
that makes you shine
with such glory?

II.

Bare mountains –
no – old grassy hills
worn out by wind
and torrential rains
shine in stark morning light
like exquisite folds
of red-brown velvet
covered with stardust.

Snow whitens the slopes
sculpted by crevices.

The earth sighs
in her sleep.

III.

I'll never tire of these mountains
made from the earth's dough
by the hands of a giant
who kneaded a cake
that was never finished,
the dough left in piles
on the table of smooth fields
surprised by their sudden end
in rich folds and falls
decorated with the icing of snow
on cloudy winter mornings.

IV.

Submerged in the sand of time,
a continent from beyond
sinks in the last sunset.

Shadows move briskly.
Soon, a gentle coat of oblivion
will cover the ridges.

The desert sleeps
devouring life.
Clocks stop.

The rocks are on fire
boiling over
into the evening sky.

Sand rises slowly.
The mountains drown
in silence.

In Passing 2

I saw another miracle today –
the jacaranda tree was in full bloom,
a purple cloud descended
or was it periwinkle?

No wonder I don't want to leave L.A.
where gardens look at the sky
with turquoise eyes of their pools,
where hills wear white scarves
of fog in the morning, where
the weight of sunshine wears me down
as I go about my daily business
of loving the world better

Eros

the   of
Angel   Desire

Eros 1

my dreams are simple –
I just want you

today, tomorrow,
in my bed, at my table – you

talking on your cell phone,
putting on your socks – you

all wet from the shower,
bewildered by the steady
glow of my love – you

touched so deeply
that it hurts – you

the one man of wicked
charm, gentle wisdom –

Eros 2

if you have a stem
that needs a flower
                I am your rose

if you are a blade of grass
that longs for the happy weight of the butterfly,
                I'll give you wings

 if you are a cherry
overflowing with rich, sweet juice,
                I'll plant you as my tree

Eros 3

my body blossoms under your fingertips
with each caress reinventing the violin

gentle curves, smoothness,
riches of a hidden voice
an instrument of delight and sorrow

fear of belonging, emptiness, absence
transformed into music

a night path through the petals,
blossoming of time – alive
waves of bewilderment
open into an abyss
of ticklish mysteries

dire loss of freedom

Eros 4

you flowered in me
with a fruit-bearing sign
of gladness

life opened its petals
smoothly rounding each now
with forever

fleshed-out in a burst
of perfection once felt
I breathed love

Eros 5

there is a rhythm
to this opening and closing
for you – with you
I'm yours – you're mine

together we'll paint
a masterpiece of loving
on the canvas
of our bodies
united in a rhythm
of summer heat
joined in timeless passion

given – taken
in a blessing
of the magic
of belonging
you're mine
I'm yours

in this rhythm
of perfection
we are one

Eros 6

we are the walnut
of perennial wisdom

locked together
(two halves in one)
we share one breath
of blessed air

delighted,
we peel the minutes
off the ancient clock

Interlude – Rivers

I. Rivers

I knew my river,
but my memory still mixes its golden sand
with the squeaky quartz crystals of the Baltic.

Vistula: a grey bandage of coolness
dressing the wounds of a forsaken land,
where Vars and Sava lived happily once
and a mermaid helped them
to defend the city from Germans.
With her shield and sword
she rose from the depths
(otherwise inhabited by the somber
and mustachioed catfish).

I know, that story is too old-fashioned
for today's bombs and bullets.
Parochial, receding into insignificance,
my childhood monster: *rzeka Wisla*.

I flew away and above. I saw –

muddy browns spread in wide ribbons,
murky waters telling tales
of Old Man Mississippi
flood the newly conquered lands –

Green embroidery coiled around
the meadows like emerald snakes,
more luminous than freshly watered lawns –

Concrete paths weaving in and out
of the city – beneath walls of graffiti
a tiny trickle brings leftovers
from the other season in L. A. –

The diamond surface of the stream
scattering riches on smooth pebbles,
to disappear amidst dry twigs
of suffocating, cricket-laden summer.

I should remember – this is California.
I should remember – I'm not at home.

II. Timelessness

Yes, there is time
Yes, there is weight
of the rocks on the skin
of the earth making
It harder to breathe
for the beast of eons

Yes, there are clouds
Yes, there is air
cut with wispy stripes
of whiteness wishing,
willing itself into being,
into solid forms that
dissolve in the merest
breeze, flee into nothing

Yes, there we are
Yes, matter stays
atoms, prions, electrons
dance in an endless cycle
of DNA spirals, molecules,
blades of grass and gravel

Yes, there is time
to watch, to catch
the transient beauty
of living in red harmony
blood circling in our veins,
rock dust changing into stars

In Passing 3

At dusk —

The waves of black clouds
rise on the horizon, ominous
like Medusa's hair

Red sun is trapped,
suspended in the snares,
useless like a hat of a dead man

It shines through the shadows,
illuminating the scorched land below
before sinking into ashes

At dawn —

The river of light
flows down the slope
towards dark contours
of pines and ash trees

A milky mist rises
above the sleeping valley
with an untold promise of
life without cruelty and horror

Eloe

the Angel

of Grief

Eloe 1

kiss me with the kiss of death
so my lips stop breathing

kiss me with the kiss of Lete
so its waters wash away
my dark memories

kiss me, so I could go in peace
to the empty fields of Elysium
for a well deserved stroll in the park
of the late graceful

Eloe 2

if I had any faith
I would worship you

your body – so perfect

now you love me
now you don't

my hope's gone now
the cult of one destroyed

your beauty – so cruel

now you hate me
now you don't

Eloe 3

life closed
above my head
like dark waters

drowning
is not an experience
I would recommend
to anyone

not even you
my old enemy
sweet deceiver

who'd have the courage
to take a deep breath
and walk under?

beyond the knowledge
and the burning guilt?

who would care
to break the surface open,
free, like you?

Eloe 4

I live a life of quiet desperation
I can't love what I have
I can't have what I love
I can't be

hours turn into days
of endless greyness
my face froze into sorrow
under the mask of laughter
I'm alone

my thoughts are filled with longing
my gestures outline the absence
of the one, living spring
of bright water –
love that could quench
my thirst for salvation

Eloe 5

burning bridges
burning, burning,
burning bridges
no way back
nor forward

pain - selfishly unshared
locked in my skull
pulsates behind the eyes

dull pretense
that nullifies everything
darkens red hues of joy
into funereal purples

my experience is
non-transferable
even words fail to capture
its omnipresent rage

Eloe 6

grief is a thief
and a stupid one at that

he stole your life
when God was not looking

(too busy –
concocting colors
to paint the canyons, stars,
dabbling in sunsets)

Interlude – Waterfalls

I. Waterfalls

Driving to the coast across Vancouver Island
along an empty, narrow canyon road,
I was bewildered by the mountains weeping.

Streams covered rock faces with long lines
flowing down like St. Peter's tears
after his denials. It was a time of despair,
of travel into darkness, unannounced.
No wonder the rocks cried with me, for me,
I cried with them.

The cheerful waterfalls of my childhood quite forgotten,
I lost the memory of winter's landscape, far away,
where ice walls surrounded thin streams of living water
longing for permanence of stalactites in the caves below.
I looked at mountain photos, white snow, graying shadows.
Who was this quiet, smiling child? Where was she now?

Soaked by thick foam that curled my hair
 into a golden halo, I survived
the wildest voyage of the Maiden of the Mist,
at Niagara Falls. I wondered about
 the honeymooners and the kitsch –
nothing for me here, no bliss, no keychain hearts.

White cloud blinded me, the roar of falling river
took me away to dreams of non-existence
that could be reached only by floating downstream
through churning waves, after becoming
one with water, one without breath.

I saw a rainbow, an echo of last rays of sunset,
more picturesque than the one on postcards,
worth every penny, even those thrown down into the falls
with just one wish that I was afraid to think or ask –
"give me serenity of death, give me peace."

II. Desolation

I found myself
on the shores of desolation.
forlorn it was –
a place few people would inhabit,
lost ones, perhaps,
who call "Death Valley" home.

The earth's brown scales
stretched into the distance –
a monster with red ridges on its back.
The hills, grey dinosaurs
with broken spines
towered above dead, salty lakes.

Pain numbed all hope.

Don't think death attractive
brought in by angels
on rainbow-painted wings.
Really, it's ugly –
limp bodies buried,
stilled hearts.

In Passing 4

I grow roses in the desert
They wither in merciless sun

Their petals, scorched by the heat,
crumble into dust
from which they came

The magic of water and light
brings them back.
Open blossoms smile at me
shyly

One after one after one
they come to make love
with the air

They shrivel to stay unchanged
clinging to life
that left them

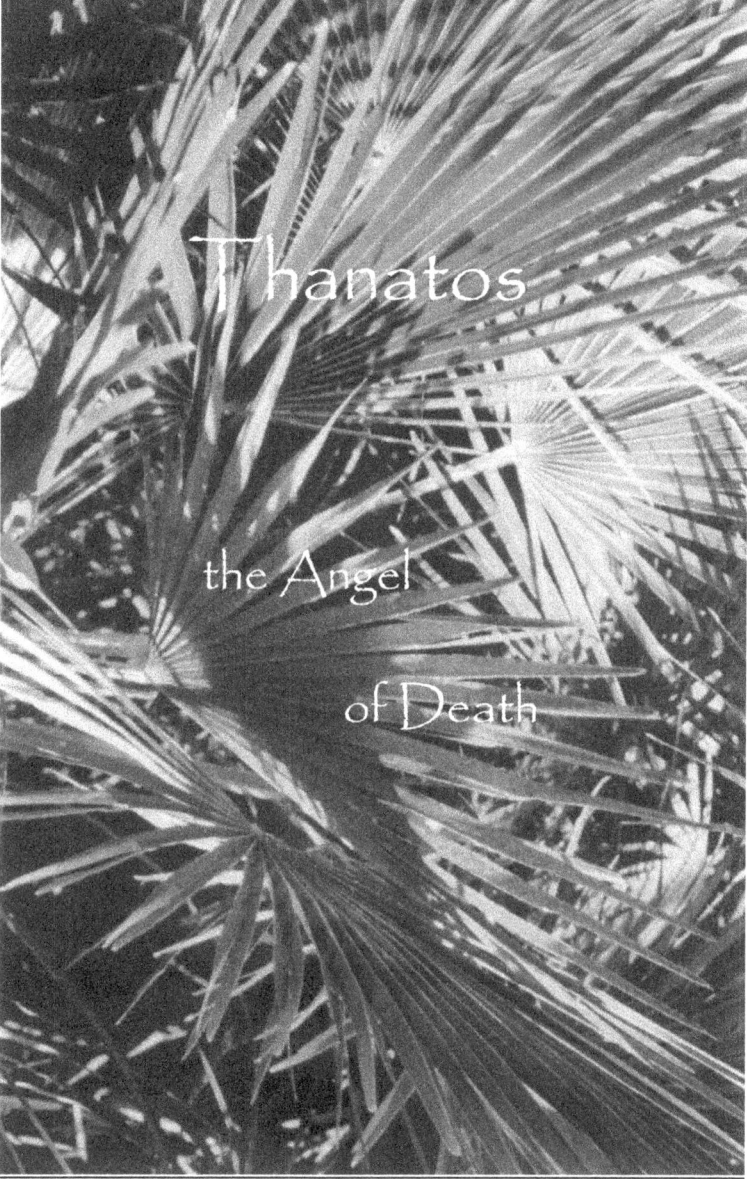

Thanatos

the Angel

of Death

Thanatos 1

how shallow the grave
how sparse the flowers
on the cement
how cold dead fingers
never to move again

how empty the home,
empty eyes, empty heart
devoid of life

we'll sing death away
we'll frighten it with incense,
we'll keep our memories
with utmost care
blocking the heartbeat
of agony that flutters
like a bird in the ribcage
before flying away
into stillness

Thanatos 2

broken pieces of fish bones
lie scattered by the tide
where sandpipers feed

hermit crabs move into empty shells
whose former inmates
lost their future, devoured

The ocean of death surrounds us
ants troop in and out of the eye
of the beetle that lies
in the middle of my path

crushed sea shells paint the beach
bone-white – prickly sand
slowly changes into rock

the fossils capture cruel snapshots
of transient past

unperturbed, we march on,
treading on traces of old tragedies

insects die first, yet outlive us
we do not mind their deaths

with a gaze fixed above,
we ignore countless incidents
of random murders, as we walk into
the gaping mouth of the Behemoth

Thanatos 3

she dreamed of his entrails
shining like garlands
festooned on the trees
along the path marked by pieces
of the plane that exploded
without burning

her dreams wove themselves
into a suffocating net
of nightmares with holes
torn by sudden flashes
of happiness when
she remembered
his laughter, his touch

Thanatos 4

grief's river
flows into the other ocean

muddy waters
carry pain's debris
into the vastness
of calm

lost, pitied,
un - forgotten

if only – oh –
if only

tears keep falling

if only – oh –
if only

unredeemable,
endless woe

Thanatos 5

white sun and white clouds
over white valley

white lilies and roses
in a wreath
on my father's tomb

white yucca flames
burn the hills like candles
of the funeral
in sparse, white air

brides are shrouded
in the white fog of nothing
they dissolve
into the holiness of their vows

widows' black
is a solid protection
from the whiteness of death
that kills colors
of life's rainbow
slowly fading into the white
skeleton of pain

Thanatos 6

pain trickles down
the solid rock of my sorrow
until there is nothing
left to hurt – a void
before another outpouring

tears don't wash away
the dust of sadness

they come and go
like summer rains –
not refreshing
in the stale heat
of despair

Interlude – Of Days

I . Dayfall

Day in, day out –
pages fall off my calendar
like overripe peaches off my tree.

I pick up each one to see how good it is.
Should I be proud or embarrassed
by the fruit of my toil?

Soft fuzz grows on spheres of juicy goodness.
Soft light of memories sweetens
long hours of endless labor.

Day in, day out, day in, day out –

II. Daydream

I dozed off in my garden,
lulled by birdsong
and the afternoon breeze
in the tree-tops. Peace
came to fill me with a sphere
of gladness. Calm stilled the air
sweetened by orange blossoms.
Each note of the mockingbird
was outlined ever so precisely
against the background
of chirping sparrows
and the random buzz
of hummingbird's wings.

Back home, on the hammock
under the pear tree, we let
the sweet pear juice flow
all over our hands and chins.
We laughed – sticky targets
for the wasps, that circled above
our heads, ready to strike, buzzing
with menace. We ran to the well
and gleefully splashed
our faces with cold spring water.
The sparrows argued by the barn;
we rested, looking at the sun
 filtered through the greenest,
shiniest of leaves. That was
 the summer of wasps and pears,
the year of danger and bliss.

III. Dragonfly Days

The California dragonflies are
as they should be – orange,
enormous, flying in formation
above green algae in the winter stream.

A hairy bug looks for a crevice
to hide his ugliness. It has crawled
straight from the pages of a horror book,
or a painting by Hieronymus Bosch –
a creature that could have been, but is not.

A blue heron floats down, his majestic wings
beat slowly until it finds a reedy alcove
for an *al fresco* dinner. Transfixed,
I watch its shape-shifting ways,
a cruel flash of movement erupting
from a graceful silhouette, standing still
as a priceless etching amidst the rocks.

Once, I knew such dark-winged herons
standing still, watching us scare away the fish
from their river with our childish giggles.

Once, red-billed storks picked their lunch
of frogs and crickets from the trail
of freshly cut grass, its straight rows measured
by the motion of my uncle's scythe across the meadow.

Like long-legged pets, they followed the man
who fed them. They paid no notice to a silent child
trying to catch a butterfly in her small hands,
watching the bright blue dragonflies
over the ditch filled with rainwater
and forget-me-nots.

Blue and orange, the dragonflies
haunt my memories, still hovering above
the smooth surface of the long forgotten stream,
beneath the tranquil expanse of high noon sky.

In Passing 5

What if there were a tree
called liquid amber?

But there is one,
a whole street of trees, in fact

Incandescent,
they spill gold and scarlet leaves
on the sidewalk
to brighten an autumn morning
among sweet magnolias
blooming out of season,
dreaming, wishing
to be stars

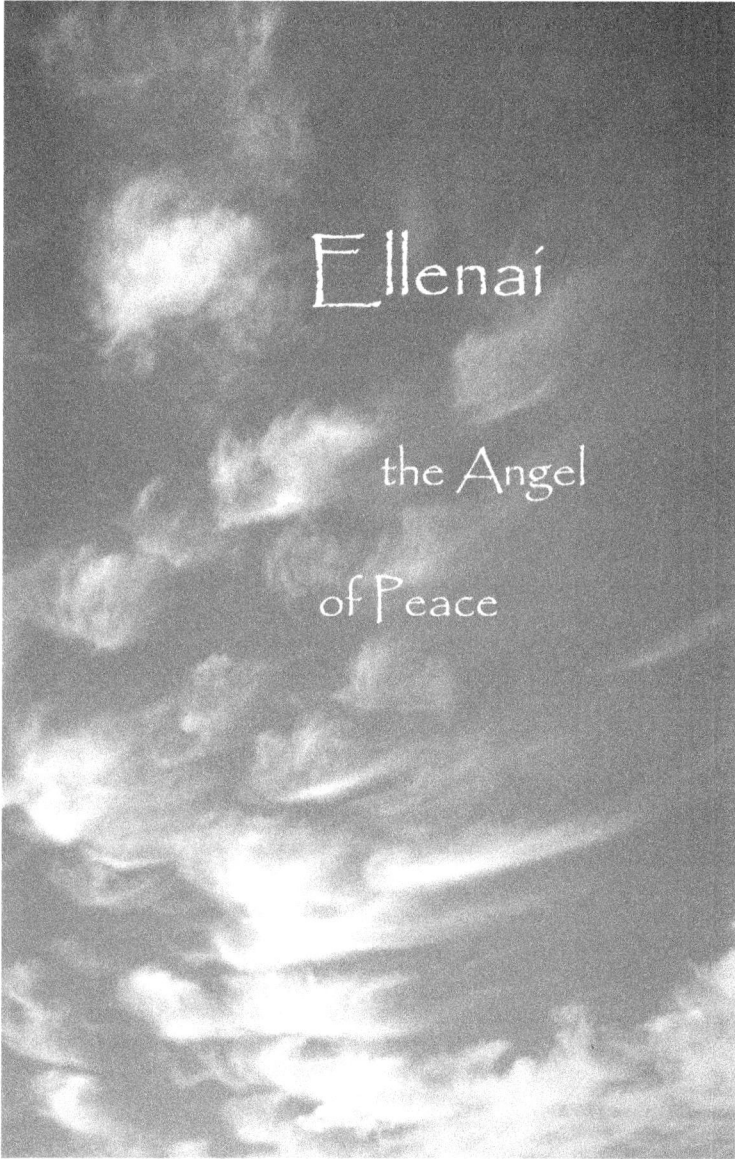

Ellenai

the Angel

of Peace

Ellenai 1

I drank the sun –
there is nothing left
for the world

I'm full of light

nobody's sweetheart
I am a universal widow
of forty four springs
and one true love

(prophetic poetry
echoes through my mind
with this messianic number)

life's winds took me
from place to place
like a rose-petal
carried by waves

I breathe the sky –
torn apart by red clouds
its blue pierced
by rays of sunset

Ellenai 2

when I dance
I become one
with the current
of the universe

I swirl like a vortex
in the cosmic stream

life flows through my veins
my body fills with delight
my hands caress the air
joy radiates
through the tips
of my fingers

do I smile?

men think me erotic
a sweetheart – a goddess
the softest of touch

Ellenai 3

breathe a song of new life
sing the song of blood
circling through your fingers
dancing in your heart –
your joy will know no limits
your ecstasy will last
now you know your promise
now you live –

the pattern's unfinished,
the spool keeps turning
weaving your colors

you make the hues
of each minute
you mix the paints

I choose the rainbow
without blemishes,
speckled with gold

Ellenai 4

I'm burning but I'm not burnt
In agony, but not yet dying
light streams out of my heart
filled into overflowing

sounds of an ancient tongue
trigger a glimpse of a time
when the rose and the flame were one
wreath of fire which engulfed me
dissolves into stillness

a white wave reaches its destiny
of nothingness
the valley brightens
under a shaft of sunlight

the air is sweetened with flutes
and harps (how obvious!)
a breath spills into silence

love is no father, no mother
but this – perfection
of all things in all
feelings collapsed into one
not a longing, really,
and not satisfaction

perfect fulfilment – all dreams

Ellenai 5

it's so nice to be
glad
contentment knows no bounds
joy
grows from the fertile soil of
tears
spilled in a happiness that
love
only could bring back from the
dead
hours and evenings beyond
bliss
merging the end with the
start
in one magnificent moment

Ellenai 6

with the noise
of unfurling wings
silence descended

turmoil within
my frightened self
dissolved
into the glass surface
of tranquil seas
at sunset

angels account for
moments such as these

love's cruel sweetness

my days are numbered

I'm caught again

emptied
of thought and sorrow

poured
into the last vessel
of midnight calm

Interlude – Of Bliss

I.

On the sandy path by the river,
step by step, with the setting sun,
I walk into bliss.

The perfect happiness of a moment
engulfs me amidst rocks, cacti
and desiccated yucca stalks.

I am a little girl, again,
coming back from the forest
with a basketful of berries.
Sand means that home is near.
I am glad. I am safe.

But bliss is more distant than ever –
a mirage on the horizon of foreign life
under a strange, turquoise sky.

II.

In a house of stained-glass cherries
you can hear a cat sleep
snoring into the comfort
of his hand-embroidered pillow.

In a house of fresh-cut roses
you can feel the air bloom
with the sweetness
of cinnamon and nutmeg.

You can taste love
mixed with raindrops
on the patio of my magic house
where everything you touch
changes into pure gold
of bliss, perfectly remembered.

III.

I'm delighted
 with the newness of this day –
          fresh, new grass and
                    fresh, new leaves and
                              fresh, new clouds
                                   in fresh, new sky
washed clean by rainfall,
colored by ever-brighter light
 of green and blue, hope and innocence,
the hues of my love.

Even the mountains wear
their fresh, new dresses
with pleats of ridges and gullies
waiting to be ironed out
by the breath of wind and time.

In Passing 6

The sun ran down the river
it smiled —

Diamonds on the fields!
Light in my hair!
Hosanna!

The sun's fingers
touched the heart
of every tree —

They grew deeper,
nourished by brilliance

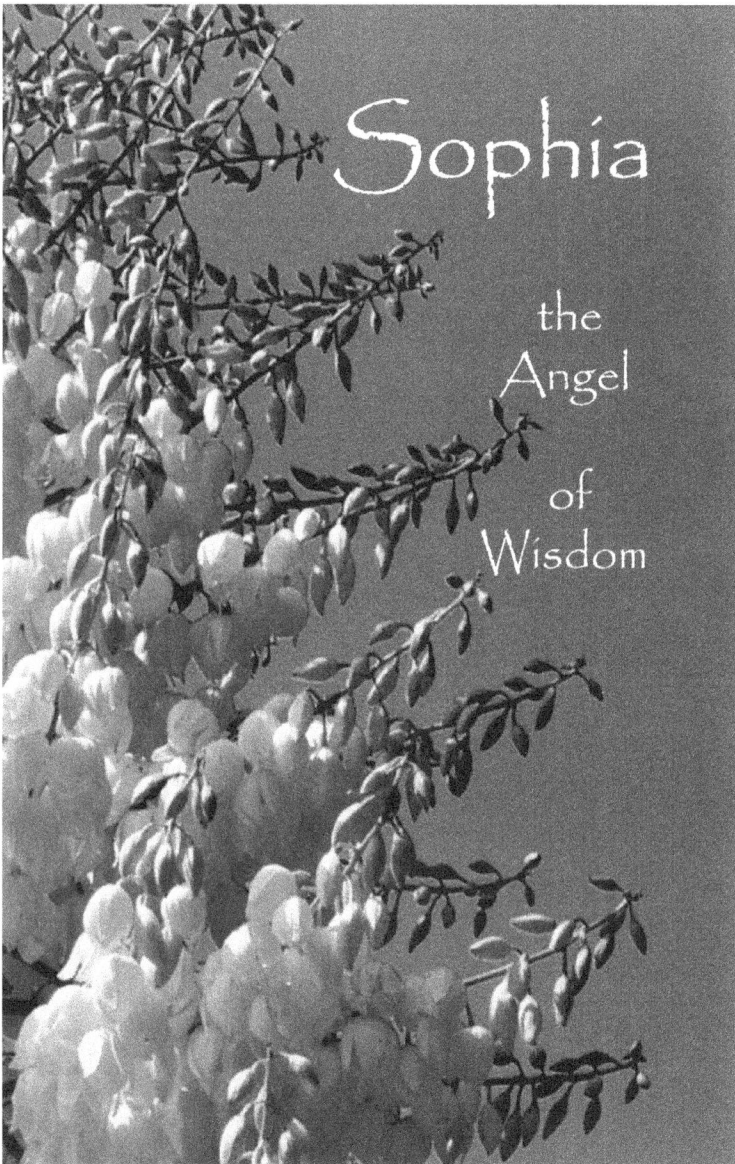

Sophia

the
Angel

of
Wisdom

Sophia 1

kiss me with the kiss
of kisses
on my lips

yes, that's better

soft roundness of the body
white circle
smooth touch of wine
on my tongue

the blood of galaxies
star clusters
flow through my veins
to the tips
of my idle fingers

my skin tingles with a new me
a glorious body
blossoms within

from bread invisible
from blood divine

a kiss a day
that's all

Sophia 2

love fell on me
like snow from high sky
gently

I stood there
waiting for
communion

I looked into the eyes
of the man
who held love
my love
in his hand

abyss called to abyss
depth touched
the deepest core
of my sorrow

my bread and body

eyes closed
"Noli me tangere"
said Jesus to Magdalene

I know
this love will shield me

I count my blessings
bless the Holy Name

Sophia 3

for a price of one life
I bought my freedom
I did it again and again

now I live as I want to

I count my delights each day
surrounded by a shield of joy
that Saint Patrick prayed for
Christ before me
Christ above me
Christ within me

the shield works
my treasure is safe,
deeply hidden, protected
in the heart of hearts

Sophia 4

oh, to float into blue distance
a dream of weightlessness,
knowledge of nothing but the air
in the lungs, air carrying the limbs
from cloud to cloud into being,
into tranquility, into peace

all made of water, we live
in the Cloud of Unknowing
we breathe a shroud
surrounding the mystical
peaks of the Ancient One
that will not be known
nor understood fully

we have to, we must fly
higher, we must grow wings,
strain in childish hope
that we'll find brilliance
hidden beyond the bluest
blue of infinity, of time

Sophia 5

you too, will find the way into the orchard
where green fruit ripens among late blossoms
I found the path, I'm waiting there already

the birds chirp and frolic among the branches
they fly – cheerful in the orange sun

you too –
the path is not too narrow,
the gate too distant

will find –
the most amazing jewel
of deep peace

the way will open soon
you will see

into the orchard of love's riches
you will come

Sophia 6

and now bless
and now
the whole, the all,
cosmos, chaos,
gleaming, living waters,
exploding spheres,
black skies filled with fire

and now bless –
blessed be the Holy,
the One beyond being,
above, below, after, breathing

now bless –
mine, ours, yours, love,
pearl strings of peace,
joy, heartbeat of stillness,
jewels of transfigured touch,
petals unfurling
into wings of glory

now blessed

In Passing 7

I am my own kingdom,
alone:
my garden's secret
you'll know
if you care to visit

we'll dance a sarabande
on wet grass
framed by blue larkspur
and morning glory

Postlude – A Vision

... see how God passes...

I.

I'm a road of white sand
stretching into infinity
the wheel of light keeps turning
within me –
faster, brighter,
still –

...mmm-hmmm...

II.

In the wheel –
I'm a spoke of brightness
a tiny flame that's ascending
into the fiery axis of the world –

... hear, hear, oh, yeah...

III.

I'm a spark shooting upwards
twirling into the vortex
an upsurge, a spiral, a lightning
follows its double ladder
of braided galaxies –

...tell us, tell us more...

IV.

A wave washes ashore
carrying me on its crest
I'm hidden in mist and foam
smoothly moving towards my secret –

a vastness seen from afar
does not frighten –

...yes, yes, praise the Lord...

V.

My hands are empty, outstretched
I have nothing to show,
no light, no treasures, no glory
no lamp to hold on to –
I'm the light –

moving from whiteness to whiteness
brighter and brighter still
carried away by the ocean
of liquid starlight –
not afraid.

...say that, say that, sister...

VI.

Stellar sand sifts between my toes
myriads of light points flicker
when I wade through knee-deep puddles
of starry paradise.
Bright spots cling to my legs
light marks my skin for the future
luminosity permeates me –
joy spills into a smile.

...he did that, oh, yeah...

VII.

I run, I fly, now I'm a kite
that rises higher and higher
into a vaster, bluer,
more translucent expanse
soaring where light beckons
ready to break the string
and escape.

...that's right, that's right...

VIII.

I sing Hosanna
on my knees.

...say ye - Amen Alleluia....

IX.

Turning, dancing,
wheels, sparks, dust of brightness
but I'm not ready –
someone pulls at the string
and brings the kite down

...hear, hear, all is right...

X.

I rise up to go humbly to eat my bread
light hidden in the crumbs
falling on everyone like manna
that covers us with a blanket
of grace – transforming
into a field of whiteness
what was us, me and many

...sing, sing, sing His glory...

...God has come...

ABOUT THE AUTHOR

Dr. Maja Trochimczyk, a native of Warsaw, Poland, and a resident of Los Angeles, California, is an author of three books of music history (*After Chopin: Essays on Polish Music,* 2000; *The Music of Louis Andriessen*, Routledge, 2002; and *Polish Dance in Southern California*, Columbia University Press, 2007) and one book of poetry (*Rose Always*, Moonrise Press, 2008). She wrote over 900 poems, she is active in the California Association of Chaparral Poets, Poets on Site, and Emerging Urban Poets of Pasadena. Her work appeared in the *San Gabriel Valley Poetic Quarterly*, *poeticdiversity*, *Magnapoets*, KRAK Group's *Sunlight Confessions*, and *Poets on Site* chapbooks for art exhibitions in galleries and museums of Southern California. She also published two chapbooks online (*Glorias and Assorted Praises* and *Poems for My Friend*).

Dr. Trochimczyk's music history work includes over 60 book chapters and scholarly journal articles, and more than 130 other publications on music and dance, including essays, dictionary entries, editorials, CD notes and reviews published in English, Polish, German, French and Japanese, in such venues as: *The New Grove Dictionary of Music and Musicians, Musical Quarterly, Lutoslawski Studies, The Age of Chopin, Computer Music Journal, American Music, Journal of Musicological Research, Leonardo,* CDs by Nonesuch and Chandos, etc. Dr. Trochimczyk is a specialist in Polish music (Chopin, Bacewicz, Górecki, Lutosławski, Paderewski, etc.), 20th century composers (Andriessen, Xenakis, Bartok, Brant) and music in the context of culture, including philosophy (musical space, the topic of her doctoral dissertation), religion (mysticism), acoustic ecology (birdsong), literature and politics. She received awards from the American Council of Learned Societies, Polish-American Historical Association, Social Sciences and Humanities Research Council of Canada, the University of Southern California, and other organizations. She is a member of the Polish Institute of Arts and Sciences of America, the American Musicological Society, and the Modjeska Club of Polish Arts and Culture, among other associations.

www.ingramcontent.com/pod-product-compliance
Lightning Source LLC
Chambersburg PA
CBHW051816040426
42446CB00007B/694